Off We Go for 80 Days

Written by

Rina & Jimin Jung

ISBN: 978-1-60594-933-8

Printed in the United States of America by Llumina Press

Library of Congress Control Number: 2012917778

For those who love to travel

24 May 2008 ~ 09 August 2008

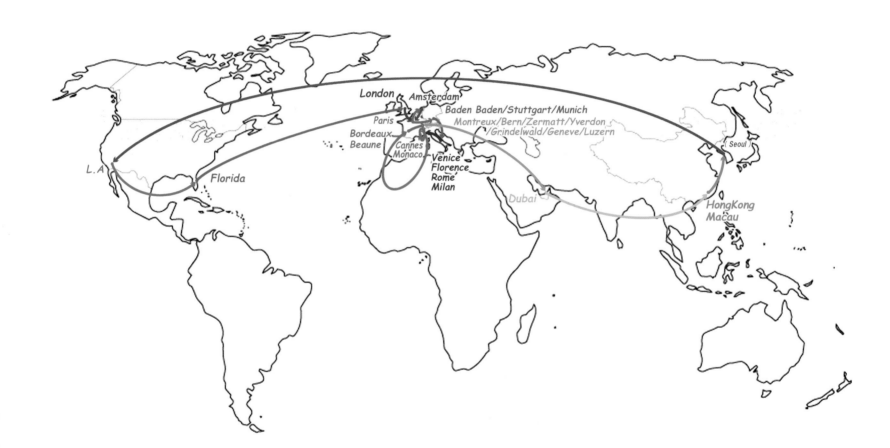

L.A

Florida

London

Amsterdam

Paris

Baden Baden/Stuttgart/Munich

Montreux/Bern/Zermatt/Yverdon
/Grindelwald/Geneve/Luzern

Bordeaux
Beaune

Cannes
Monaco

Venice
Florence
Rome
Milan

Dubai

Seoul

HongKong
Macau

Itinerary for 80 days.

May 24...New York/ London	Buckingham Palace
	Royal Mew
May 25...London	Lego Land
May 26...London	Horse Back Riding at Hyde Park
May 27...London	Tennis Camp
	Big Ben, London Eye
May 28...London	Tower of London
May 29...London	Tennis Camp
	Shakespeare Globe
May 30...London/Paris by Eurostar	
May 31...Paris	Eifel Tower
	Louvre Museum
	Champ Elysee
June 1...Paris	Notre Dame Cathedral
	Musee d'Orsay
	Sacre - Coeur
June 2...Paris	Shopping
June 3...Paris/Amsterdam	Diamond Factory
	Anne Frank House
June 4...Amsterdam/Paris	Zaanse Schans
	Windmill Village
June 5...Paris	Golf at Disney Golf Club
	Versailles Apartment
June 6...Paris/Mulhouse by TGV	
June 7...Mulhouse/Basel	Art Festival
June 8...Basel/BadenBaden	
June 9...Baden Baden/Vogtsbauernhof	Frellichtmuseum
	Cuckoo Clock Factory
June 10...Baden Baden/Stuttgart	
June 11...Stuttgart	Mercedes Benz Factory/ Benz Museum
June 12...Stuttgart/Munich	BMW Welt
June 13...Munich/Fusen/Munich	Newschwanstein Castle
June 14...Munich	Marien Platz
	Crystal Museum
	Science Museum
June 15...Munich/Venice	Saint Marco Plaza
	Rialto Bridge
June 16...Venice	Murano Glass Factory/ Glass Museum
	Burano
	Chess Playing at Bridge of Academia
June 17...Venice/Florence	Ponte Veccio
	Uffizi Galleries
June 18...Florence/Pisa/Florence	Pisa Tower
	Galleria Del Academia
	Salvatore Ferragamo Museum
	Gilli Cafe
June 19...Florence/Rome	Trevy Fountain
	Spanish Steps
	Shopping at Via Condotti
June 20...Rome	Vatican Museum
	Coloseum
June 21...Rome/Milan	Duomo
	Shopping at Via Monte Napoleone
June 22...Milan/Monaco	
June 23...Monaco	Petit Train in Monacoville
	Monaco Beach Club
June 24...Monaco/Cannes/Biot/Monaco	Cannes Petit Train
	Red Carpet
	Marine Land

June 25...Monaco/Bordeaux by Air	Cafe de Paris
June 26...Bordeaux	Winery Visit
June 27...Bordeaux/Paris	Grand E'picerie de Bon Marche
June 28...Paris/Beaune	Bisho
June 29...Beaune	Romanee Conti
	Cote de Beaune/ Chambertin
June 30...Beaune	DownTown
July 1...Beaune/Montreux	
July 2...Montreux	Summer Camp at Monte Rosa
July 3...Montreux	
July 4...Montreux	
July 5...Montreux	
July 6...Montreux/Bern/Montreux	Einstein Museum
	Alpine Museum
July 7...Montreux	
July 8...Montreux	
July 9...Montreux	
July 10...Montreux	
July 11...Montreux	
July 12...Montreux	
July 13...Montreux/Zermatt/Montreux	Zermatt- Mattehorn
July 14...Montreux	Summer Camp - Crossbow and Archery
July 15...Montreux	Chillon Castle
July 16...Montreux/Yverdon Les Bains	Pestalozzi Museum
June 17...Lausane/Evian	Olympic Museum
	Evian Factory
July 18...Montreux/Grindelwald	
July 19...Grindelwald	Jungfraujoch
July 20...Grindelwald/Brienz/Geneve	Ballenberg Open Air Museum
July 21...Geneve	Soccer Camp
July 22...Geneve	Soccer Camp
	Flower Clock/ Jet de Eau
July 23...Geneve	Patek Philippe Museum
July 24...Geneve/Zurich	Red Cross Museum
July 25...Zurich/Luzern/Dubai	Swiss History Museum
	Transportation Museum
	chapel Bridge/ Lion Statue
July 26...Dubai	Sky Dome at Emirates Hall
	Wild Wadi/ Bruj Al Arab
July 27...Dubai	Dessert Safari
July 28...Dubai	Gold Souk / Burjman/ Wafi
July 29...Dubai/HongKong	Tsimshachoi Shopping
July 30...HongKong	Sampan Ride
	Victoria Peak
	Dimsum Restaurant
July 31...HongKong/Macau/HongKong/Macau	
Aug 1...HongKong/Seoul	
Aug 2...Seoul	Coex - Korean Culture Festival
Aug 3...Seoul	Coex
Aug 4...Seoul	KyungBok Palace
Aug 5...Seoul	Kayaguem Factory
Aug 6...Seoul	Dragon Spa, Kayaguem Lesson
Aug 7...Seoul	Book Store
Aug 8...Seoul/L.A	L.A Tour/ Hollywood
Aug 9...L.A/ Orlando	

United Kingdom

London

Buckingham Palace

Royal Mews

Lego Land

Horse Back Riding at Hyde Park

Big Ben

London Eye

London Taxi

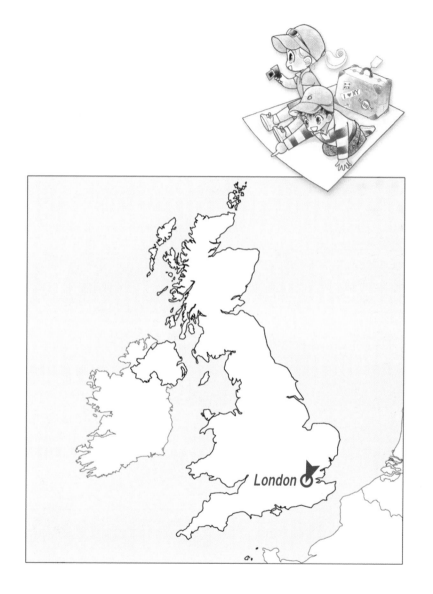

London

Buckingham Palace—*J.J*

Our world trip began in London, and our first stop was Buckingham Palace. We saw the cool changing of the guards! I liked the humongous horses security rode. With just one step, I bet they would break you into smithereens!

Buckingham Palace—*R.J*

When I finally arrived at London, I felt a pang of excitement in my body. Our schedule for today was to go to Buckingham Palace. After the taxi dropped us off, we went to see the changing of the guards. It was spectacular! The guards were wearing fuzzy looking black pom poms on their heads, and they were marching like robots. I kept clicking my camera to take pictures. My favorite part was when the guards were exchanging interesting movements with the Congo guards.

Pom Pom

Royal Mews—*J.J*

Next stop was the Royal Mews. I was so happy to walk next to the Queen's carriages. I thought the royal family was rich 'cause their carriages were all covered in gold! Then we went into a gift shop, and I bought a British guards' PJ.

Royal Mews—*R.J*

Before we went back to the hotel, we went to see all of the Queen's carriages at the Royal Mews. Mom made a reservation for us to get in before we left for the trip, so we had no problem getting inside.

Although all the carriages were pretty, we loved the carriages covered in gold with lots of ornaments the best. I wondered if they were made with real, solid gold.

I was imagining the king and queen riding them, waving hands.

Luxurious

Lego Land—*J.J*

Lego Land was fantastic! I got to race cars with Rina at the Driving School. I was trying so hard to step on the accelerator to go faster than Rina who was driving in front of me. It was fun. And I saw a lot of technology, too, especially at the Lego Miniland. So cool! All the things were made out of Legos and they actually moved! I really wanted to make the same miniland at my house, too!

Lego Land—*R.J*

We had to make several train transfers from London, but I was excited about Lego Land. When we got off the train, there stood Windsor Castle. Instead of peeking inside the castle, we rushed to Lego Land by taxi. As we entered the entrance, I saw the big Lego Land sign, and that made me more enthusiastic. Our first stop was the Lego

Unbelievable! Lego pieces!?

Land Driving School where I got a driver's license. It had my picture on it and looked like a real driver's license like my parents have. Then we went to the digger challenge. There, we got to control a mini bulldozer!

It was so cool. I did not know how to maneuver the gears, but people watching me showed me in gestures how to work it out. I dug out a pile of balls, lifted, and dumped them at the other place. After that, we went to the fire academy. We had to pump a handle to move the fire truck and then manage to shoot water.

It was fun, but everyone who did it was panting when they got out. So was I. Miniland was unbelievable. They built several cities of the world out of Lego pieces. Boats and cars moved around, though they were made out of Legos! The Build + Test was cool, too. We got to make cars of our own with Legos. The best thing about it was racing our cars with other kids. Lego Land was awesome!

Big Ben—*J.J*

Big Ben is the symbol of London. When I saw it in the picture, it was small, but when I saw it in life, it was humongous! When the government officers are working at night, the lights are turned on. Big Ben was AWESOME and BEAUTIFUL.

Big Ben—*R.J*

We went to see Big Ben, the clock tower in the Palace of Westminster. I always wanted to see Big Ben after reading about it in *The Magic Tree House*. It was marvelous. When I first saw it, I wondered if it was covered with gold. My mom told me it could be gold leaves. I was speechless. It looked so luxurious and graceful.

Horseback riding at the Hyde Park—*J.J*

In London, we rode horses in Hyde Park every day even when it rained. One day, it rained so much, and my hands got frozen. My horse was my best friend. His name was Buddy! I trotted with Buddy, and I loved Buddy!

Horseback riding at the Hyde Park—*R.J*

It was raining, but fortunately horseback riding was not cancelled. We first went to Hyde Park Stables to meet our horses and instructors. I was very surprised at how small it was. It was on the north side of Hyde Park on a very narrow street paved with cobblestones. I could smell the horses as we got near the place. After waiting a few minutes dressed in our boots, hats, and gloves, we finally rode our horses into Hyde Park.

It was very muddy and rainy, but the horses didn't seem to mind. When we were far enough into the park, we started trotting. I was scared at first, but then I got used to it. We had to stand up in the saddle and then down, up and down many times. I was bouncing at first, but I got the hang of it. It was like a tour. I got to see Rotten Row and the Serpentine.

I thought Rotten Row would be stinky but it wasn't, not like its name. The Serpentine was right next to Rotten Row. It looked like a giant serpent. No wonder they named it like that. But it was awesome riding a horse in Hyde Park! I looked forward to doing it again and again.

London Eye—*J.J*

The London Eye is a Ferris wheel, except it is much bigger and has 28 capsules. The inside of each capsule was huge and all of it was clear glass. The Ferris wheel moved slowly, but inside, I didn't feel like we were moving at all! And from inside, I could even see Buckingham Palace. A helicopter was landing there.

London Eye—*R.J*

As we crossed the Westminster Bridge from Big Ben, I saw a beautiful Ferris wheel… the London Eye! It was huge! And it is very different from the typical ferris wheel. Each compartment is a glass capsule, so we could see a 360 degree view. It was very pretty. I could not believe that I was actually there. I only knew about the London Eye from my science homework a month ago. It was so exciting that we got to ride it!

There were many other people inside the same capsule, but I did not mind. I squeezed in between people so I would not miss the wonderful view of London, and I took pictures.

I was so happy that I even let my brother mess with my camera. It was a thrill of a lifetime.

London Taxi—*J.J*

The London Taxi has a round shape that reminds me of a pear. Inside, it was plain and bold. I was a little scared because there was no seat belt. When the taxi stopped all of sudden, I jerked forward into the driver's seat. The London taxi was not my favorite.

London Taxi—*R.J*

The cabs here in London were very different from the ones in New York. In New York, cabs are yellow. Here in London, they are mostly black in a round and antique-like shape. I liked the interior of the London taxi. It had more space than I imagined, and "No Seatbelts Inside" was like a treat for me. We rode the taxi to get to Buckingham Palace, and I asked the driver what company made the London taxis. I learned that the taxis are manufactured in London by a British Company called LTI (London Taxi International).

No other company is allowed to make British taxis. I understand now that this is how the British people can preserve the tradition of these unique looking taxis. I think it was a good tradition for them to keep. It symbolizes London very well.

Cool London Taxi ♡

France & Monaco

Paris
  Eiffel Tower
  Louvre Museum
  Versailles Apartment
  Le Grand E'picerie of Bon Marche

Bordeaux
  Bordeaux Airport
  Bordeaux Wineries

Monaco
  Monaco

Cannes
  Cannes

Beaune
  Beaune Burgundy
  Hospices de Beaune

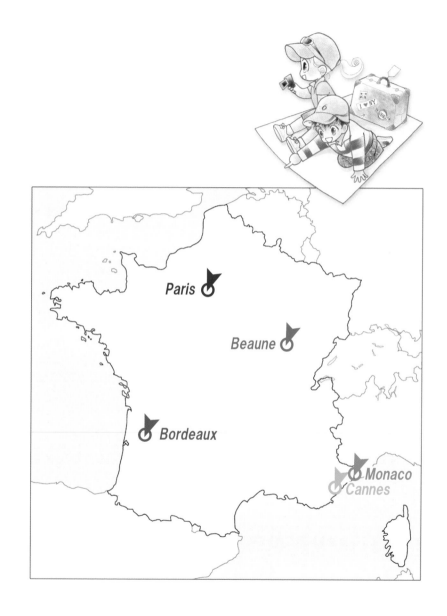

Eiffel Tower—*J.J*

The Eiffel Tower is big.
First, I thought it was made out of wood. But I was wrong. It was really made of iron. I learned it is the symbol of Paris, and it stands 1,000 feet high. There were lots of people taking pictures and people selling stuff. The best part was eating popcorn at the foot of the tower.

Popcorn is the best!

Eiffel Tower—*R.J*

I learned that it was once called the "Awful Tower" by those who disliked it. It was the first tower made of iron in the middle of many stone buildings. There were several plans to knock it down because it was not considered pretty. However, it is still standing and has even grown taller, with an antenna on top. We didn't get to go inside, but we took lots of pictures.

There were many people in the area, picnicking and taking pictures like us.

Iron Tower.......
Pretty though...

Louvre Museum—*J.J*

France! Whoo Hoo !
We visited a huge palace with a clear pyramid. I thought it was a palace, but French people call it the Louvre Museum. There were millions of people. Inside, we saw the Mona Lisa. She looked sad. I think it's because she doesn't have any eyebrows. As we walked, I saw a lot of people around Venus de Milo, too. She looked weird without her arms and hands. But my sister said she is beautiful. Anyway, people don't have the same feelings and opinions.

No arms and hands?

No Eyebrows?

Louvre Museum—*R.J*

Inside the museum, I saw the real Mona Lisa. I liked her mysterious face. I took lots and lots of pictures. Venus de Milo also impressed me. When I saw the face of the goddess, I was astonished about how detailed her face was. I loved her eyes the best. They looked so soft. I took a lot of pictures of her. Then we went to the private chamber of Napoleon III. We saw beautiful furniture and carpets of royal blue. I was guessing that the Emperor liked the color blue like I do.

What a beautiful eyes!

Mysterious Mona Lisa!

Versailles Apartments—J.J

Inside Versailles Apartments, there was a Hall of Mirrors. It was a pretty room filled with gold, crystals and mirrors. I was amazed. It was so beautiful. I thought Louis XVI was a rich king. I also liked the king's bed with its curtains. I wish I could have one like that, so I could have privacy. I loved the gardens at Versailles. We went around the gardens in a golf cart. It took us more than an hour to go around.

King's Bed is my favorite!

Versailles Apartments—*R.J*

We took a taxi from Paris to the Versailles apartments. It was an enormous castle. The moment I saw it, I knew it was something very special. We took the private guided tour inside the private chamber of Louis XVI. The apartments were so beautiful. The furniture looked so luxurious with lots of glittering gold and detailed carvings. The draperies were all velvet and silk with embroidered gold.

There was a bathroom used by the king, which was hidden behind the stove. The only thing I thought strange was the size of the bed. It looked so tiny and high above the floor. The room that was used as a ballroom was called Hall of Mirrors, and it was so pretty with many chandeliers from Venice. I was day dreaming, wondering who had been there at the parties held by the king.

We also drove to where Marie Antoinette used to live. We didn't get to see inside of it 'cause it was being renovated, but we saw the gardens of Petit Trianon. On the way to Petit Trianon, I saw beautiful gardens which had been the dream of Louis XIV. That also was spectacular, but much too grand to walk in.

On the way back to where we return the cart, I felt like I was in a maze as we went through the groves. It didn't feel that way when I was up on the 2nd floor of the Versailles apartment peering down at the garden. But the actual size was like a hunting ground.

While we were heading back, we saw many beautiful statues in the fountains. One of them had Nymphs of Winter and Summer. I liked Marie Antoinette's garden the best. It had such nice smelling roses and a pretty pond. After we returned the cart, we bought some books about French History .

Le Grand E'picerie of Bon Marche—*J.J*

In Bon Marche, I saw a crystal bottle of water. It said "Bling," and it cost 25 Euros. 25 Euros is almost 40 US Dollars! It was pretty though. We bought a soccer ball trophy bottle. I pretended to be a soccer player!

Le Grand E'picerie of Bon Marche—*R.J*

sugar   cute and pretty   wine

We stayed in Paris again for one last visit. Before traveling from Bordeaux to Burgundy, we decided to stay one more night in Paris. I felt like I'd been living there my whole life.

I remembered every street, shop, and station we had been through on our last visit.

Since we went to Bordeaux, we became very interested in wine. So we went to a very interesting grocery store called Le Grand E'picerie of Bon Marche. They had a huge wine selection. One even came in a mini carton and looked like a milk package with a straw. They also had a cheese corner, a bakery, and a water corner. The water corner was very interesting. One bottle was shaped like a soccer ball; another had crystals on it. I do not think anyone would want to buy it because it was almost US $40. I saw chicken, duck, and turkeys with their heads and tails on with feathers. The moment I saw them, I ran away from the corner.

When we explored some more, we saw nicely shaped sugar and grape jam in a tube, which my brother and I thought it was a body cream. There was also handmade chocolate in little handbags. They were all very cute and pretty. My brother bought water in a soccer ball and I bought a mint refill. Mom bought jam in a tube. I was hoping to come back the next day. There was too much to see inside the store.

Bordeaux Airport—*J.J*

I went to Bordeaux by airplane and right after I got there, I immediately noticed that the Bordeaux people like wine. 'Cause there were grapevines just outside the airport building. I really wanted to pick the grapes!

Bordeaux Airport—*R.J*

After we ate breakfast at the Cafe de Paris in Monaco, we went swimming in the hotel pool. It really felt good to swim in the morning. The pool was salt water and had a beautiful harbor view of Monaco.

Then we headed to Nice to take a flight to Bordeaux.

In front of the Bordeaux Airport building, there was a small vineyard. I could see some grapes but they were still very tiny. I thought it was a good idea to plant grapes at the airport because that is what Bordeaux is famous for.

I was very excited to think of visiting the Bordeaux wineries.

Grapes in the airport?

Bordeaux Wineries—*J.J*

Today, I went in a black limousine to four wine châteaux. The first one we went to was the Lafite winery, which means little hill in French. The wine cellar was dark, cold, and spooky. There were oak barrels all over. The smell was a mixture of oak and wine. It smelled great. My mom said she liked the aroma, too. Wineries were fun to visit. I liked smelling the wine the most!

Bordeaux Wineries—*R.J*

We visited four wineries today. First, we went to Château Lafite Rothschild. The word, 'Lafite' means 'Little Hill' in French. And Rothschild was a family. The Rothschild family owned two wine estates. Lafite and Mouton. When we entered the winery, we saw huge oak barrels storing wine. Next we saw how they rank and fine the wines. It was really interesting to see how they rank the wines. They do it with candles to see the sediments in the dark wine cellar, comparing one barrel to another. Then we were shown the private cellars of the Rothschild family. I saw thousands of the old dusty bottles they own. At last, we did some tasting (not me and my brother though). The person who guided us prepared a 1995 vintage wine! What a surprise. We did the same thing at Mouton. But at Château Margaux and Château Haut-Brion, we were able to see how they make the oak barrels. And at Château Haut-Brion, we saw lots of stainless tin vats lined up in the fermentation room. This winery used stainless tin vats for fermentation instead of huge oak barrels.

When we got back to the hotel, we were tired. I told my mom that I felt sicker and sicker. By the time I got to the Château Haut-Brion, I felt like I was going to throw up. I guess I smelled too much wine today.

Monaco—*J.J*

Monaco is a very clean place. The ocean was clean and the houses were beautiful with lots of Ferraris and Porsches on the streets. For Europeans, I learned it is a dream place to visit. I went to the Monaco Beach club. I enjoyed the diving board way up high. It was like sky diving! I wanted to dive again and again!

Then I went to the ocean just next to the beach club. I could see millions of fish in the deep blue ocean. There were some tiny fish and big fish too. My dad bought a net for me to catch the fish. I thought I would catch some fish, but I didn't. I tried and tried until my shoulders got sunburnt.

Monaco—R.J

After traveling to France, my favorite thing to do is to eat croissants with butter and jam together with English breakfast tea. The croissants we had were fresh from the oven and were very good.

We took a walk to old Monacoville. Monaco is a very beautiful city with views of the Mediterranean Sea. It is very hilly, and there were many escalators connecting streets that were down the hill to streets on the upper hill.

When we got to the top of the hill and close to an aquarium, we saw a petit train touring Monaco. So we rode on it and passed many famous places. We even passed where the F1 race was being held. When we got off, we walked all the way to our hotel. It was a lot of fun walking. We passed a Farmer's market and met an old woman who bought us a delicious bunch of wild strawberries. I have never met such a kind person in the USA.

After returning to the hotel, we got ready to go to the Monaco Beach Club. The beach wasn't what I expected. I thought it would be a nice sandy beach but instead, it was full of rocks and pebbles. But they had a man-made small beach for the little kids to play. The ocean water was very clear. When we saw fish swimming and kids catching them, my dad got a net and let us catch some. We couldn't catch any, but in the end, we went to the big pool and did some diving. It was a lot of fun. Monaco was paradise!

Cannes—J.J

Cannes is the city of the film festival. Many people were acting like actors and actresses on the red carpet. I posed like one, too. I kind of felt like an actor. We toured Cannes with a mini train. Cannes was beautiful with many sand beaches.

Cannes—R.J

We visited the city of the film festival called Cannes. We ate breakfast in one of the cafés on La Croisette. Then we decided to ride on a small train touring around Cannes. As we were walking to the petit train, I saw a man working on a giant sand sculpture on the beach. He was making a car. I asked him how many days he has been working on it. He said it took him two days to make the car. And he said he only used sand and sea water. It was awesome. I wanted to know more about what he was doing, but Mom was waving us to come to the train.

On the petit train, we were able to go on to the top of the hill to take pictures of Cannes. Cannes was beautiful, with lots of flowers, sandy beaches, and cute looking houses. When we got down the hill, we went on the red carpet where all the famous people walk during the film festival. It was really fun to pose on it. I felt like a celebrity.

Beaune, Burgundy—*J.J*

In Burgundy, we went to a vineyard called Domaine de la Romanée Conti. It is famous and makes the most expensive wine. I learned that grapevines grow from the rock. The more the root suffers, the better the wine tastes!

Beaune, Burgundy—*R.J*

From Lyon Station we took TGV to the Burgundy Region. We changed trains in Dijon and soon we were at Beaune. Beaune was beautiful with lots of vineyards. First, we climbed up to a hill to take a picture of the beautiful view of Burgundy. On that hill was the Virgin Mary watching over all the vineyard. We have seen many wineries but the best and most famous of them is Domaine de la Romanée Conti.

It was on a very small piece of land with rocky soil. I was surprised at how expensive the wine is. $10,000 and up per bottle. The last stop we made was at a small Domaine. There, my brother asked if people washed their feet before stepping in the grapes for wine-making.

The answer was "NO". We were all very surprised. Our guide explained that there wasn't any need because the alcohol cleans everything. I am a little disappointed. My fantasy of wine making is kind of disappearing.

Hospice de Beaune—*J.J*

The Hospice de Beaune, I learned, was like a hotel for sick and poor people. I thought some day I would help the poor people. I thought God would like my idea. There were many compartments with red beds and they looked comfortable. I wanted to lay down and see for myself how it feels!

Hospice de Beaune—*R.J*

Hospice de Beaune was a castle for the sick and homeless. Nuns took care of the sick, and the sick had a chapel to go to. The most special thing to me, was the roof and the stream running below Hospice de Beaune. There was a glass window on the floor to show the stream running under the Hospice de Beaune. It shows how they keep the building clean.

Keeping the building clean

 # Netherlands

Amsterdam

Anne Frank House
Zaanse Schans

Anne Frank House—*J.J*

Since my sister really wanted to visit Anne Frank's House, we went to visit Amsterdam. I was a little scared of the black windows and the Nazis. The rooms were so small. I couldn't imagine living in that space!

I felt goose bumps crawling up my body. When we watched a movie about Anne Frank, I felt like the Nazis were really gonna come. Anne Frank died when she was twelve years old because of those mean, grumpy, and bad Nazis. It is a very sad story. I wanted to cry.

Anne Frank House—*R.J*

As we entered the house, I wondered where the toilet and Anne's room was. Well, I soon found out after climbing up the stairs to the secret annex. I could not believe I was standing where Anne Frank and the Nazis had been. There were lots of videos showing and pictures of Anne. I felt really sorry for Anne. And there were thousands and thousands of people visiting the house. I was wondering what could have happened if Anne had not been sent to the camp or had survived the camp. Would she be this famous? I thought she got this famous because her life ended in tragedy.

What if she Surrived?

I bought several books about her, which are sold only in the house museum, not elsewhere. My brother and I started to read the books right after Mom paid for them.

It was interesting to know more about the sufferings of the people during the Nazi regime.

Zaanse Schans—*J.J*

The last day in Amsterdam, we went to a windmill village called Zaanse Schans. Inside, there was a yummy cheese farm. I saw goats and chickens and lots of other animals, too. We went inside a windmill and climbed up and down the stiff ladders, which made me think I was gonna break my arms or legs. We also went to a clog workshop. Clogs are wooden shoes that were worn by Netherland people a long time ago.

My first impression was that the clogs stink when they are wet. The shape was kind of cute. I learned that they will get lighter when they are dry, and it takes six months to dry the shoes. I am glad I got a pair for myself.

Zaanse Schans—R.J

Although it is outside of Amsterdam, we decided to visit the Windmill Village, Zaanse Schans. Mom told me that there used to be 700 windmills but there are only 7 left, now. Inside the village, there was a cheese factory and a clog workshop. We bought smoked cheese and aged cheese. The ice cream tasted delicious and milky. When we finished eating, we went inside

So cute!

a windmill. To get the better view of the top part of windmill, we climbed the wooden ladders that go up and down. I thought I was gonna die. It was so steep. But it was cool. With only the power of wind, flour is made. It is amazing.

The last shop we went to was the clog workshop. We even got to see them make the clogs. A man demonstrated how to make a clog from the piece of wooden block. He made a hole in the block and shaped the corners to look like a shoe. Then he showed us how much water is still inside the shoe. In order to use it as a shoe, it has to be dried for six months. There were many beautiful clogs painted in different colors, I wished I could get the prettiest one. My brother and I got the fresh wooden clogs that had just been made for one Euro. I can`t wait to paint them when I go back home.

 # Germany

Baden Baden

Black Forest and Cuckoo Clock

Stuttgart

Mercedes Benz Factory and Museum

Munich

BMW Welt and Museum

Neuschwanstein Castle

Deutsches Museum

Black Forest and Cuckoo Clock—*J.J*

We went to a village near the Black Forest in Germany. The people like to make stuff out of wood in the Black Forest. I saw people making Cuckoo clocks: "Cuckoo, Cuckoo." The Cuckoo clock has a paper bag inside that opens and shuts. That makes the sound of the clock. We bought a Cuckoo clock for about 1,000 Euros. I was so happy that we bought a cuckoo clock.

I wanted to put more animals in it, like a fox, dog, horse, or cat, etc. But my parents said it does not have any extra space. Too bad.

46

Black Forest and Cuckoo Clock—*R.J*

From Baden Baden, Germany, we hired a taxi to go to the Black Forest. As we went on our way, we passed many pretty wooden houses. I felt like I was in a picture painted by Claude Monet or some kind of artist.

Mom kept saying it was so pretty, and that almost all the houses had flowers decorating them outside on the balconies. We all agreed with her.

When we got to our destination, Freilichtmuseum in Vogtsbauernhof, we knew we had a lot to see. First, we went to the cool traditional black forest house. We kept on exploring the old houses. One was built in 1599 and one had Jesus on a cross surrounded with tools. It was really funny.

Then we made a cuckoo flute. I loved it. We even made a stand for it. People in the Black Forest were very skillful in wood craft. It was so cute.

Even though I liked that place, I had to leave it for our next stop, which was the famous Cuckoo clock factory. There we met the owner, and he showed us how to make the Cuckoo clock. I learned that it is a long tradition and it has been passed down through six generations. The great thing about visiting the factory was buying one for our home. We chose the one with the golf player swinging his club to beautiful music. I can't wait to see it in my house.

Mercedes Benz Factory and Museum—*J.J*

We went to the wonderful Mercedes Benz Museum. It was huge! But the factory was much much better. It was tremendous. It was cool to wear goggles through the tour, so the fire sparks won't get it in my eyes. But one touched my shoe, and I thought my foot would burn, but it was okay. I loved the factory, especially the humongous engines. Vroom Vroom!

Mercedes Benz Factory and Museum—*R.J*

The exciting place in Stuttgart, Germany was the Mercedes Benz Factory. The actual factory! It was awesome. First, we went to the body shell making of the S Klasse. Mostly in that part of the factory were robots shooting laser of super glue onto the body shell pieces to attach them. We wore safety glasses to make sure we were safe from the laser. At first, I was scared of the sparks from the fire, but then I got more used to it as we walked along the safety zone. I loved the part where they did the final touches because we got to see how they put in the dashboards, doors, roofs, and a lot more. My brother was so amused that he kept staring until we had to call his name three times! It was a great experience, and the Benz museum near Stuttgart was another great place to explore.

As we passed all the models in the Museum, we came to a one that was originally named the Mercedes Benz. I learned that Karl Benz named it after his 11 year old daughter. It was great to learn history. After all, I felt like the Mercedes Benz is the best car in the world ever.

BMW Welt and Museum—*J.J*

In Munich, we visited the BMW Welt. It had a lot of games. I enjoyed making my own car. I played car racing, too. And I joined a very, very interesting kid's program. It was so much fun I didn't notice an hour go by. What fun it was! I wanted to buy one or two of the BMW cars, but I bet they are very expensive. I used to like the Ferrari, but now I don't know whether I should get a BMW or a Ferrari.

It will be a tough decision to make.

BMW Welt and Museum—*R.J*

After we arrived in Munich, we went to the BMW Welt. We were supposed to go to the museum, but it was closed due to renovation. Instead, we visited the Welt, which was right across the street from the museum. The place looked ultra modern and high tech. It is a double cone shaped building with lots of simulations and BMW models displayed inside. So cool and a lot of fun! We could play with lots of machines inside such as car racing, hydraulic pressure, and sailboat racing. We could even design our own cars.

Mom signed us up for the Junior program, and in that lab, we got to try things like explosions, reactions, brake disks, and a lot more. What I liked the best was the Reaction part because we could try using a brake pedal to stop. Everything was so cool there.

BMW Building

Cool!

We were given a BMW access card, and before we started any simulation game using the machine inside, we had to swipe the card in order to start it. I am going to treasure the card forever. I thought the BMW factory had the coolest stuff of all the car factories I've been to.

Neuschwanstein Castle—*J.J*

To the Castle! I took a train for two hours to a village called Fussen, Germany. I could not believe the castle was on top of the mountain. The view was so BEAUTIFUL from the top. I thought that King Ludwig did a great job building the castle. I was really interested in the bridge that hung from the canyons. I could see the beautiful castle in front of me. We got on a little horse carriage that led us to the top, but I did not enjoy the ride at all. `Cause the horse butts were right in front my face when they pooped!

But I learned the horses had a big job to do getting stones for the castle. Mom said Walt Disney got an idea from the castle. I thought it looked a lot like the one in Disney World.

Looks like Disney Castle!

On the mountain top Great job!

Yuck

Neuschwanstein Castle—*R.J*

System kitchen hundred years ago?!

"Wake up! We might miss the train to the castle," Mom shouted.

We were planning to visit the castle that had been drawn as Sleeping Beauty's Castle by Walt Disney. Neuschwanstein means New Swan Stone in English. The castle was built by King Ludwig II of Bavaria. He had only been able to build one third of his dream castle, and he lived in it for only 172 days. He was found dead in the lake, but no one knew what had happened to him. I wanted to know more about it and did not mind the two hour train ride to the foot of the mountain. The castle was located on top of the mountain, so we took a horse-drawn carriage to the top. Two horses pulled the fully loaded carriage over the steep roads. I guess the horses were very tired, so they pooped a lot while walking. I felt so bad for the horses.

But that is how they had carried the stones and materials to build the castle. Inside, the castle was very different from the one in France. More simple. And instead of using real gold leaf, some gold was just paint. I saw a lot of wall paintings of the Bible stories. Although I didn't like King Ludwig, I liked his belief in Christianity. He designed his own praying room. I liked that idea. I wanted to know more about King Ludwig, so I bought a book and read on the train back to Munich. I think he was a little different from others as well as a bit mad. He was smart enough to make an elevator inside the castle and a modern system in the kitchen more than one hundred years ago.

Deutsches Museum—*J.J*

Feeling like a hamster! I went to the Deutsches Museum. I heard it was the oldest and largest science museum in the world. The children's section had a lot of things to play with. There was a gigantic wheel. It had a green and red lights that told it when to stop and when to go. It rolled so fast when I pushed it, I felt like I was a hamster.

The museum was filled with cool stuff. Even in the shop there were a lot of things. I wanted to buy the solar powered bike. It was so COOL!

Deutsches Museum—*R.J*

We went to the world's largest and oldest Science Museum. They had a lot of different things, but I liked the mining exhibition the best. It was actually like a real mine! It was dark, and we had to descend into the underground tunnels.

There were wagons that carried the minerals through the tunnels. There weren't any gems in it, but it made me feel like I was actually inside of a mine. It was an awesome feeling.

My next favorite spot was the museum shop. It was very big with lots of interesting goods. I bought rocks again in the shop: agate, rose quartz, and citrine.

This mine is great!

Love Gem Stone!

 Italy

Venice

Night Train to Venice
Saint Marco Plaza, Venice
Glass Factory, Murano
Playing Chess in Venice
Gondola ride Venice

Florence

The Tower of Pisa
Salvatore Ferragamo Museum

Rome

The City of Rome(Trevy Fountain)
Vatican Museum
Coloseum

Milan

Duomo Milano

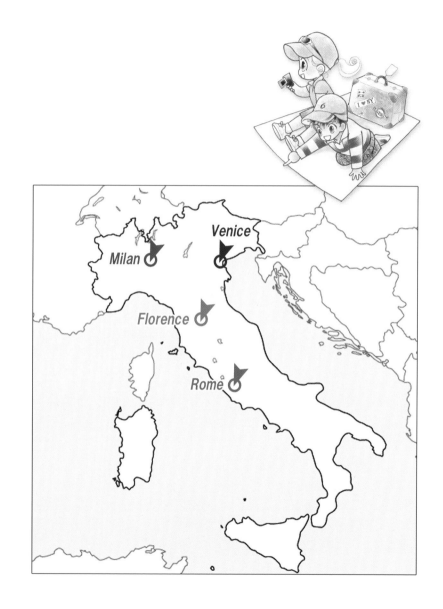

Night Train to Venice—*J.J*

We are off to Venice. We rode a night train. The cabin had a bed and sofa. It was so comfortable. I thought it was a camping train. It was so so so so cool. I wanted to live on that train!

Night Train to Venice—*R.J*

When I arrived in Venice, I was very relieved that I didn't have to sleep on that terrible train. Although my brother said he slept well and loved the train, I woke up several times. The cabin had two beds and a sofa, so my dad and I slept in one cabin, while Mom and Jimin took the other cabin.

At first, I slept in the upper bed, but soon after, I tucked into my dad's bed. Still I could not sleep well with the noise from the other cabins and the noise from the train, and the concern about robbery.

The cabin had a lock, but it still did not make me sleep good. I thanked God we arrived safe in Venice.

Saint Marco Plaza, Venice—*J.J*

Before I knew it, pigeons were on my shoulders, head, and arms! Pigeons were all over the Saint Marco Plaza in Venice. They looked so dirty. I put food on my clothes, and I pulled my sleeves down, so they wouldn't get on my skin.

Some brave pigeons landed on me. My dad helped me by throwing chips at them. A lot of feathers dropped from the sky like rain. Tons of pigeons flew near me. It was F.U.N.

Rain of feathers!

Saint Marco Plaza, Venice—*R.J*

We took the water taxi from the Santa Lucia Station and went to Saint Marco Plaza. We saw the Basilica where one of the Disciples of Jesus was preserved. It was beautiful with such great detail. As we passed the columns of the Basilica, we saw a flock of pigeons. People were feeding them. It was a pigeon crazy place. I got so sick, I wanted to leave the place as soon as I could.

But my brother loved feeding the pigeons and insisted on staying longer. I begged him to move to another place. I felt so sorry that the beautiful place was polluted with dirty pigeons and pigeon poop.

Glass Factory, Murano—*J.J*

Today, we were planning to go to a glass making factory. The water taxi was waiting for us in front of the hotel. I was glad to ride the water taxi again. I kept talking and chatting with joy in the taxi. After a short ride, we got to a factory called CAM.

There were masterpieces of colorful glass. It was marvelous. Inside the factory, even though I was ten yards away from the fire, it was super H.O.T. My nose and cheeks became red and sore.
I learned that glass
making is hard work.

super HOT!

Glass Factory, Murano—*R.J*

Early in the morning, we took a water taxi to go to the Island of Murano to watch glass blowing. When I entered the factory, I saw the master and apprentices working together. They were making a goblet with a long stick. They put the stick into the furnace and took it out, shaped it, and put it back into the furnace. I knew the furnace was very hot, 'cause I could feel the heat from about 30 feet away.

Beautiful!

The furnace was 1,700 degrees. I thought the workers had to be very patient and hardworking to continue shaping glass under such hot conditions.

The next place we went was the glass museum. I saw many interesting glass works, like a wine glass with disappearing lines. Once the glass is filled with liquid, the lines disappear. There were chandeliers, and glass that was made especially for the kings and queens, and a lot other statues made of glass.

I liked them all. They were so beautiful. I wish I had some of them in my room. The factory staff gave us some little souvenirs to take home. I chose Snoopy riding in a gondola. So cute and lovely.

Playing Chess in Venice—*J.J*

Today, I saw two men playing chess near the Bridge of Academia in Venice. I joined, too. The man pointed at me, asking if I wanted to play. At first, I thought I was going to win, but gradually, I lost. I kept saying in my head that I needed to practice more.

Playing Chess in Venice—*R.J*

After we had some refreshments in the hotel Gritti Palace, we crossed the Bridge of Academia to get a good view of the canal. Jimin found a group of people playing chess there, and he wanted to watch them. I wanted to go someplace else, but he would not leave the place and stood like a statue with several other adult groups watching the players.

Very proud!

Then finally, I found him sitting across from a man with curly hair playing chess together. He eventually lost the game, but Dad seemed to be very proud of him playing chess with an Italian adult. Jimin seemed to enjoy it a lot.

Gondola ride, Venice—*J.J*

Venice is filled with gondolas. It is so low, narrow, and long that people use a long stick to push it. Sometimes, they sing songs while riding on the boat.

We saw Mozart's house and the Rialto bridge. The houses in Venice had water under them. The water looked mucky. But I thought it was a good protection from the jewelry burglars.

Good!

Gondola ride, Venice—*R.J*

Before we left the hotel, I wanted to take one last walk through the alleys. I complained that I did not get a chance to ride a gondola. It was early morning, so I could not find many gondolas nearby. Usually, they were everywhere on the canals. We walked to Rialto Bridge, and Mom found a gondola man mooring his boat. He let us on his Gondola for a short ride. I was excited. As we went under a bridge, I looked at my jacket and noticed pigeon poop on it. It was on the front and back. What a disgusting feeling! I could not enjoy the beautiful views from the gondola because of the pigeon poop. But my dad told me to care about more important things and enjoy the ride. After all, that is what I have been nagging them about.

Pigeon Poop~~!! Yuck

First, we got to see Mozart's house, then Casanova's house. The place there looked really small. Last we saw Marco Polo's house. Mom told me who Marco Polo was. I got interested in reading more of his story. Everything was great except the pigeon poop.

The Tower of Pisa—*J.J*

The Leaning tower of Pisa. We were leaning against the Leaning Tower of Pisa. It really really leaned. I almost fainted! The Pisa tower was built as a bell tower, my mom told me. When Rina went up the tower, I wanted to go too, but those meanie people said "NO." I had to be eight to go up to the top. Two more years. I was so jealous!

So jealous!

The Tower of Pisa—*R.J*

We just made it to the train to Pisa before it left Firenze station. After we arrived, we took a bus to the entrance of the Leaning Tower of Pisa. When I saw the Tower of Pisa, it was smaller than I expected. I imagined it to be as tall as the Eiffel Tower. I learned that the Tower of Pisa was built as a bell tower. I even got to walk up the stairs to the top. While climbing the circular stairs, I felt so dizzy that my head hurt. The angle of the stairs made me feel like I was falling down. But I made it to the top with my dad. Dad was supporting me and encouraging me all the way. From the top, everything looked so small. People on the ground looked like ants. When I tried to take a picture of my mom and Jimin on the ground, I could not get them on my camera. They looked so tiny.

My brother could not get into the tower because of his age. He needs to wait until he's eight years old. So Mom stayed down below with my brother. My head was filled up with how it did not fall despite how it leaned. There was a video showing how people had been able to stop it from leaning further. I am glad it went successfully. More people should come and visit this marvelous tower.

Salvatore Ferragamo Museum—*J.J*

There were millions of shoes in the Salvatore Ferragamo Museum. I learned shoe making was Salvatore Ferragamo's favorite thing to do. Salvatore Ferragamo was very creative. He made lots of shoes in different designs. He even made shoes that looked like it was for prisoners. They had some spikes, but they were high heels. They looked very special.

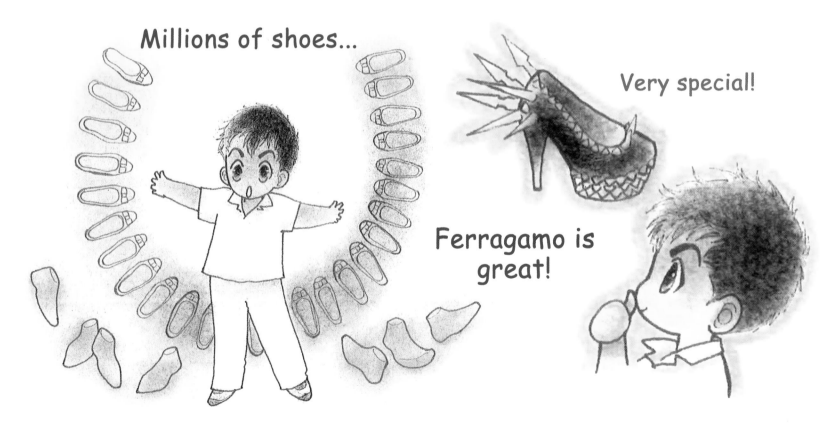

Millions of shoes...

Very special!

Ferragamo is great!

Salvatore Ferragamo Museum—*R.J*

I saw many different kinds of shoes. I liked the one with the stacked squares the best. I was impressed to know that Mr. Ferragamo knew his destiny was to make comfortable shoes. And knowing his destiny, he continuously improved the shoes he made for many celebrities and others. I was touched by his work.

Mr Ferragamo knew his destiny...

What about my destiny?

The City of Rome—*J.J*

The Romans loved fountains. I found fountains everywhere I went. I wondered if the Romans built the Trevy fountain to attract tourists. There were so many tourists. We couldn't find a spot to stand at first, but luckily we got a place right in front of it. I was glad to be able to watch the fountain up close.

The City of Rome—*R.J*

We left Firenze and headed to Rome. On our way to Rome, I read a book about Michaelangelo, and his works of art. By the time I finished reading it, we were in Rome. First, we ate lunch, and we went to the Trevy fountain. When we got there, we saw people sitting on the steps like flocks of pigeons. Luckily we found a little bit of space where we could stand, and we were able to take pictures with the famous fountain.

Next, we walked to the Spanish steps. I learned that the steps were called Spanish steps because on the top of the stairs lived the Spanish ambassadors. Down on the famous street --Via Condotti--I saw a very impressive Louis Vuitton store. It had the best display, with illuminated moving stairs. So far, I thought Rome was great, with beautiful shops and grand fountains.

Vatican Museum—*J.J*

Early in the morning, we went to the Vatican Museum where the Pope's treasures are kept. There were many gold, sparkling, and shining treasures. I wished I had one of these treasures. We went to the Sistine Chapel, and we saw Michaelangelo's famous painting. I was so impressed with how he worked on the ceiling for four years!

In Saint Peter's church, I lit a candle and prayed! I saw an unusual heart-shaped light coming through the window.
I think the light came through just for us. I thought it was a blessing from God!

Blessing from God!

Vatican Museum—*R.J*

When the taxi dropped us off at the Vatican Museum, there was a long line. We followed the line in, and we were told that the line could stretch out around the entire wall. We were early, so the line was not that bad. As we walked to different places, I could not believe how many treasures the Popes had owned for generations. There were sculptures, bathtubs, maps, tapestries, silverware, jewels, etc. We finally came to the Sistine Chapel where Michaelangelo worked by himself for four years painting the ceiling with fresco. It was such a beautiful place. The guards kept telling people to be quiet. But people kept taking pictures and whispering about how beautiful it was.

I liked Saint Peter's Cathedral the best because it was pretty and had lots of bodies preserved. It even had St. Peter's body. We prayed in the chapel, and it was very calm and relaxing. Before exiting, I saw a heart-shaped light on the floor. It was coming through the window. On the floor, it was shaped like a heart. I wished my Catholic friend was here to see it.

Very calm...

Many treasures!

Colosseum—*J.J*

Today we went to the Colosseum, and it was huge. I couldn't believe the gladiators fought here with tigers and lions. I felt bad for the animals ,which are now endangered. I imagined the hungry lions and tigers coming after me. It was so cruel. I felt as if dark, mean, hungry eyes were staring at me. When the crowd put their thumbs up, it meant to save the gladiator, and thumbs down meant to kill him! I wanted to learn more about gladiators.

Colosseum—*R.J*

The Colosseum is a huge stadium that soldiers, slaves, and gladiators fought in. I could easily imagine the blood of humans and animals flooding the floor of the Colosseum. 5,000 animals were slaughtered every day. I felt bad for the animals.

The Colosseum was ruined by the people who took the marble stones to build other structures after the Roman Period. But it still looked beautiful today. Mom bought some more books about the Colosseum and Roman History. We wanted to read the books right away, so we found shade inside to sit and read. It was a very hot day in Rome, but the shade in the Colosseum was surprisingly cool without any fans or air-conditioning.

Still beautiful!

I wanna know more about Roman history.

On the way back to our hotel, my dad said, "We saw places where people were saved and where people were killed in the same day. The Vatican was the place saving people's lives, and the Colosseum was the place killing people."

Duomo, Milano—*J.J*

Milano is the city of fashion. I saw movies of fashion shows on a big screen on every street corner. The Duomo in Milano is so sharp looking. It looked like it would go right through my hands! They call it a Gothic style church. I thought it looked like 100 spears flying right into me.

100spears!

Duomo, Milano—*R.J*

When we were inside the Duomo, Sunday mass had already started. As we looked around, we saw many columns. My brother and I wanted to light the candles inside the Duomo, so we did that and prayed. Outside, we saw many gargoyles and statues. It was really a pretty sight.

Next, we went to where all the famous brands were. The Via Monte Napoleone. We got to see the headquarter of Armani and the Bvlgari café as well. Both were really pretty. The Armani shop was the biggest one I had ever been to. And it was fun looking at the beautifully designed clothes.

 Switzerland

Bern
Bern and Einstein Museum

Zermatt
Zermatt- Mattehorn

Montreux
Chocolate Train & Gruyree Cheese
Archery and Crossbow
Chateau de Chillon

Yverdon les Bains
Pestalozzi Museum

Grindelwald
Jungfraujoch
Ballenberg Open Air Museum

Geneve
Soccer Camp, Geneve
Patek Philippe Museum
Red Cross Museum, Geneve

Luzern
Transportation Museum
Lion Statue, Luzern

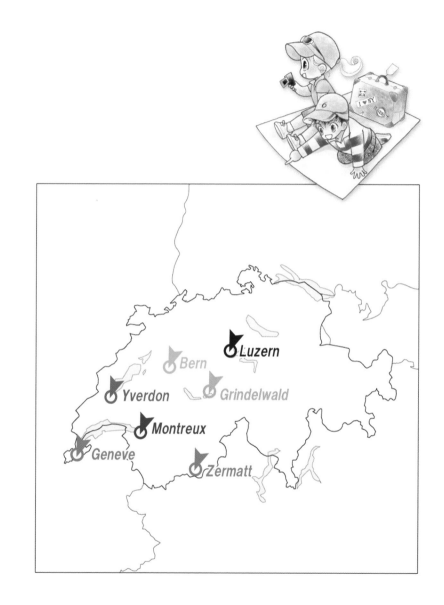

Bern and Einstein Museum— *J.J*

Our train ride to Bern was two hours. I really liked going on German trains. ICE is the name of the cleanest train I ever been on! The minute we reached Bern, I noticed that there were lots of arcades. These were good shelters from rain or snow, but they were as old as Grandpa! We walked a lot looking for a trumpet store. But we walked for nothing 'cause all the shops were closed on Sunday. Wa Wa Wa!

I liked the Einstein museum, next to the history museum. They displayed weapons from the Middle Ages in the front yard. I was anxious to try one of them and I did. Yipee! Not only that, we also learned a lot about Einstein's life. He was a very famous scientist. He created a theory about relativity. It's like if one train is moving and you are riding one that is not moving, then you feel like you are moving. I still don't get why people are crazy about it.

Why peple are   crazy about Einstein?

Bern and Einstein Museum— *R.J*

When we arrived at Bern, I felt really excited about visiting the capital of Switzerland. I imagined it would be a busy city, full of life. I thought everything would be noisy and we would have a lot of things to do just like in New York or Tokyo. But I was wrong. It was calm, and quiet, and many buildings were

connected with something like a roof on the pathways called an arcade.

It was a nice place to walk even when it rains or snows. Since all the shops were closed, we enjoyed window shopping. Little shops along the arcade had lots of beautiful things in the windows.

After our walk, we went to the Alpine Museum and the Einstein Museum. They were just across the street from each other. In the Alpine Museum, we saw things like tools to climb the Alps, maps of the Alps, and we watched the video about Alpine climbing.

I liked the Einstein Museum better because we learned about Einstein's life. I saw the notes that Einstein used and his picture during his school days. Outside of the Einstein museum, they displayed many weapons of the Middle Ages because the History Museum was next door. My brother was anxious to try all of them. I liked Bern a lot.

Zermatt—J.J

Zermatt is the village of no cars, so it was safe to walk around. If you are tired, there are horse-drawn carriages to ride. We went off to see the Matterhorn. It is a triangular shaped mountain that is the symbol of Switzerland. I wonder if the chocolate, Toblerone, is shaped like the Matterhorn. It tastes sooooooo good!

    We went up the mountain by train, but it was too foggy to see the Matterhorn. Instead, God sent us an Ibex! It was even better than the Matterhorn, I thought.

Zermatt—R.J

As soon as I woke up, we went to the Montreux station to go to Zermatt to see the Matterhorn. It is the symbol of Switzerland. We were very unfortunate because it was cloudy and rainy. We changed the train in Visp to Gothard Bahn which was clean and pretty. The train ran through

No horse poop at all!

Clean air!
Clean street!

valleys, mountains, and tunnels. I saw lots and lots of chalet style houses with flower pots hanging from the balconies. They were really pretty; I was busy taking pictures. When we arrived at Zermatt, we saw a lot of Japanese tourists. I saw several horse-drawn carriages waiting in front of the station to load their luggage. Mom told me that Zermatt is a village free of cars. I did not see any except a tiny hotel shuttle operated by battery. So people either have to walk or ride a carriage. The hotel shuttle is mostly used to carry bags for the tourists. I felt Zermatt was a very safe village with clean air. Although there were carriages around the village, I was surprised not to see any horse poop on the street.

After lunch, we went up the mountain on the famous Gonergrat Bahn. If it had been a clear day, we would have seen the Matterhorn from the train window. But we could only see gray clouds and fogs. When we arrived at the last stop, we went to the highest mall in the world. While we were up there, we saw a mountain ibex climbing down on the rocks. The place we were standing was 3,000 meters above sea level. I thought it really was a miracle to go up the mountain 3,000 meters on a train.

After we came down, I realized I hadn't been able to breathe well up in the mountain. I had that funny, dizzy feeling. Later, I learned it was called mountain sickness. Before we returned, we went to the Alpine Museum that was in the middle of the town. In there I saw the rope used by the first conquerors of the Matterhorn. The rope they used was very thin. I could not believe they climbed such a high and steep mountain with that thin rope. No wonder it broke while they were descending from the Matterhorn, killing three people. This Alpine museum was far more interesting than the one in Bern.

Chocolate Train & Gruyère Cheese—*J.J*

Early in the morning, we took a chocolate train to a cheese factory and the chocolate factory. Inside, the train was antique, and I was surprised to see that breakfast on the train was all made of chocolate: chocolate croissant, chocolate cookies, and even hot chocolate! The seats were velvet, and the numbers were painted gold. I also learned that it had been put together from old trains. The train's bathroom was my favorite place in the whole wide world 'cause I could see the bottom of the railroad! Then the train took us to a cheese farm. I learned to milk a cow and about how Swiss cows eat different herbs in the Alps. My favorite cheese is Mammoth Cheddar cheese, but my mom likes Gruyère cheese.

After that, they took us to the Cailler chocolate factory. We got to eat a lot of chocolate. It was yuuuummy, but pretty soon, I got sick of chocolate. I wanted to throw up. They shouldn't give so much chocolate for tasting.

Breakfast!?

Railroad!

Hot chocolate

Chocolate bar   Chocolate croissants

Chocolate Train & Gruyère Cheese—*R.J*

When I arrived at Montreux station, I was excited because it was the day that I was going to go on the chocolate train. After we found the track number and boarded the train, we got our seats and took pictures inside and outside the train. We found out that the train was an antique. But they decorated it nicely. The bathroom was interesting. If people pee there, they don't have to flush because the pee goes down on the ground! People can even see through it.

A few minutes after the train started, they served us hot chocolate. Well, they had a choice of hot chocolate, coffee, or tea, served with chocolate croissants and chocolate. Everything was chocolate. It was really a nice breakfast.

When we arrived, we went to the Gruyère cheese factory and saw how to make cheese, and where to store the cheese after it's made. There were

Good tastes!

displays of different plants and herbs in the Alps that Swiss cows eat everyday. We were able to smell them. I understand now why the Swiss cheese and milk taste so good. We also got to enjoy an audio guide on how to milk cows. We bought some cheese, too. Gruyère cheese is big and made in a round shape. People use it to make fondue. I loved the taste.

After we saw the cheese factory, we went on a bus to Gruyère's village where we visited Château de Gruyère which means Castle Gruyère. Even though, it was a castle, it had no king or queen ever lived there. It had been owned by a count. I was really shocked to know that a castle that big wasn't lived in by kings and queens.

Next, we went to the Cailler chocolate factory. We saw the making of chocolate, the cacao beans used to make it, and we tasted it too. Then we went on the train to go back.

Archery and Crossbow—*J.J*

In summer camp in Switzerland, I tried the crossbow, but I only got 9 points. I felt terrible. The crossbow is simple to use, like a gun, but it shoots arrows instead of bullets. I was relieved that it wasn't firing anything. The crossbow weighs as much as me. When I shot it, I thought I would faint. It weighed a zillion pounds. Archery was much, much better and easier.

Archery and Crossbow—*R.J*

In Switzerland, we tried crossbow and archery for the very first time. First, we did the crossbow. It was like a gun but with arrows. It was very cool and very heavy. Holding it steady was hard, and shooting it at the target was even harder. Next, we did archery. It was not easy at first, but then I got the hang of it. Once I knew how to do it, it was actually fun. I liked when the arrow launched into the air. Some people won medals, but I didn't. It is nothing to complain about. After all, I needed to get used to it, and it was my very first time. Although I didn't win anything, I still had a lot of fun.

91

Château de Chillon—*J.J*

Chillon Castle was very old but clean. It was on the shore of Lake Geneva and had a moat just like other castles. It was close to Monte Rosa, our summer school. I liked the bathroom the king used. 'Cause I could peek at the lake water. The poop goes down three stories below to Lake Geneva. There were two holes, one for the king and one for his friend. They poop while they chat! I wanted to do the same thing!

They poop while they chat chat chat!

Château de Chillon—*R.J*

We went to Château de Chillon after summer camp in Monte Rosa. It wasn't a winery like Bordeaux. It was a castle built on a small island very near the shore of Lake Geneva. I had been seeing lots of pictures of Château de Chillon in magazines, brochures, and post cards. It looked very beautiful on the outside, and it was a lot of fun to explore inside the castle. My favorite place was the king's bathroom. There were two big holes, one for the king and another for his friend. The king in this castle invited his friends to join him in the toilet. It sounded very funny. I could see the long drop from the toilet hole to Lake Geneva. It went all the way down to the lake. I thought it was very convenient to have a toilet that dumps things into the lake. I also explored the basement that once was used as a prison for Bonnivard and saints. I tried to find the footprints of Bonnivard, but I couldn't. We walked back along the shore of Lake Geneva and peeked in on a jazz festival in Montreux on our way back.

Toilet hole to Lake Geneva!

Bonnivard footprints???

Pestalozzi Museum—*J.J*

The Pestalozzi Museum was in a protected castle. The castle was used for the Pestalozzi school for the poor. I heard Pestalozzi lived like a beggar so the beggar could live a better life. I don't think I could sacrifice my life like Pestalozzi. I don't want to live like a beggar, 'cause beggars look dirty.

Oh no ×
I don't want to get dirty...

Pestalozzi Museum—*R.J*

Yverdon-les-Bains was a 15 minute train ride from Lausanne. We went there to visit the Pestalozzi museum. I saw his room and his pictures. Mom told us what his accomplishments were. He started a school for the poor children in the castle of Yverdon-les-Bains. It was the first school for the poor. I thought Pestalozzi was a smart person like Albert Einstein. He lived like a poor man to help the poor live better. I thought it was a great idea. The design of the castle was very unique. The building was square with a patio in the center. I imagined school children running around the patio.

A smart person after Einstein...

Weird design!

Jungfraujoch—J.J

We were planning to go to Jungfraujoch! We took two trains. The first train was OKAY, but the second was too crowded. We were packed like a sardine can. I found some space around the legs of an adult standing; it was roomy and comfortable sitting on the floor between those legs. I really didn't like that train. Bleh! The top was freeeeeezing cold. I thought I would turn into a ice cube, brrrrrr! I saw snow covered mountains, and huskies were waiting to take people on a ride. I was excited to ride the sleigh pulled by the huskies, but it was too short. I wanted to ride more! But I had to say bye bye to those cute huskies. I gave some pats on their backs.

Too short!

So fun to touch!

Then, mom took us to an ice palace. It was all made of ice, ice seals, ice fish, etc. I slid through the ice tunnel. I couldn't stop touching the ice. I think the Swiss people did a great job on the tunnels.; train tunnels in the mountain and ice tunnels in the glacier. After having fun at the ice palace, I went to send a postcard to Mrs. Eveland, my best teacher. I hope she will like it.

Jungfraujoch—*R.J*

Europe's highest viewing place is called Jungfraujoch. We had to change trains once in Kleine Scheidegg. When we rode the second train, we had to stand because there were too many people. It was most tiring when we entered a long tunnel that went through three tall mountains. I learned that a man had a dream to make trains go straight through the mountains instead of going around. It is amazing that he made his dream come true.

When we arrived at Jungfraujoch, I saw snow covered mountain peaks up close. They looked like giant tents. After we looked around the Sphinx Observation Terrace, we went outside to play in the snow. I couldn't believe I was walking on snow in the summertime at Jungfraujoch, Switzerland.

As we walked, we saw huskies waiting to pull the next person, and we wanted to try it. At the beginning of the ride, the huskies ran as fast as they could, but toward the end they slowed down. The ride felt lightning fast. But it was so much fun. We then went inside the building to eat lunch and mail the postcards, which will have a stamp that says the "Top of Europe." I thought it was so cool.

We also went to the ice palace where I saw many sculptures made of ice. We could even skate inside the ice tunnel. My brother and I tried sitting on the ice bench, and I felt my butt getting very cold. We wanted to stay a little longer, but our heads began to hurt because of mountain sickness.

Ballenberg Open Air Museum—*J.J*

I liked the Ballenberg Museum a lot, especially the goats there. One came running to me. It was a baby; he or she was so so so cute. He even climbed on me. I wish I had a goat for a pet. He jumped on my lap and bit my shirt. I didn't want to leave him. He followed me until I had to go. Tears came to my eyes. In the museum, there were old Swiss houses. And there were lace making people, and basket weaving people, but I liked the animals the best.

Ballenberg Open Air Museum—*R.J*

We said goodbye to Grindelwald, took our luggage, and went on a train to the Ballenberg Open Air Museum near Brienz. When I got to the museum, I saw a stuffed cow on display. It was really weird because it even had the poop, too. The museum showed different houses built in Switzerland and showed how the Swiss people lived.

The houses were all very pretty. They were made of wood and decorated with flowers. They were very similar to the ones we saw in the Black Forest in Germany. We walked a little bit on the trail, then we ate German style sausages, took pictures with the goats, and visited the houses. In the houses were wood carvers, cheese makers, and cheese container makers. I could tell the houses were pretty old because they were damp and dusty. Some of them were 500 years old. After looking at all the houses, we came to where there were piglets. Their hair felt very rough., not fluffy at all, surprisingly. Then we went to a basket weaving area; that was cool. They have to soak the wood with cold water before using it. The man weaving the basket was very quick at it. If we had more time, I would have wanted to try it. But we had to rush back to Geneva.

Soccer Camp, Geneva—*J.J*

We joined a soccer camp in Geneva. We played a lot of matches, and our team won almost every game we played. I made many friends. One of my friends was called Alexandra. He was my best friend in soccer camp. He scored all of the goals, and we won all of the games. Thanks to him. I think I will be as good as him when I'm eight.

Win every game!

I think I will be as good as him at eight.

Soccer Camp, Geneva—*R.J*

When I woke up, I was nervous because I was going to join a soccer camp for the very first time. When I got there, I was even more nervous. I walked onto the soccer field and introduced myself to the coach. She showed me some drills. I learned how to turn, step, and stop the ball. We had a lot of matches, too. I also made friends.

One of them was from the Czech Republic. After making some friends, I started to feel more comfortable. Soccer camp seemed really short. I could not believe I was there for seven hours. When I was done with soccer and met my mom to go on the bus, I told to her that I really had fun. I realized that I was already looking forward to doing it again the next day. I learned that anything for the first time can make me nervous. But once I do it, I feel very confident.

At first, very nervous

Once I do it, very fun.

Patek Philippe Museum—*J.J*

I went to the Patek Philippe Museum. There were a zillion clocks. They were made with gold, silver, and pearls. I wanted to buy one, but it was just for display. I was surprised to hear that it had been made 200 years ago. There were so many watches. I felt my eyeballs go round and round. Mom told me that the Swiss are famous for watch making.

My eyeballs went round and round...

Patek Philippe Museum—*R.J*

Mom said we are going to visit a watch museum since we were in Switzerland. It was in downtown Geneva. As we entered the building, up the stairs, there were watch making machines displayed.

I was surprised to know how old they were. Mom told me that watches told the status of people long ago. The old ones were really pretty. Almost all of them had pearls and gold on them.

Next, we went to the modern section. I liked the modern watches because they used more leather. On the same floor, there were two very cool clocks. One of them had Moses. When the figure tapped the rock with his stick, a small river flowed inside the clock. It was amazing. I learned that Switzerland is famous for making clocks and watches.

Red Cross Museum, Geneva—*J.J*

At first, I thought the Red Cross Museum was boring. But when I found out more about it, it was so cool. They started the Red Cross by helping wounded soldiers. I saw the cruelty caused by war. I saw pictures of many one footed men and women injured by bombs. I wanted to volunteer to help.

It's more fun than I thought...

Red Cross Museum, Geneva—*R.J*

Our last day in Geneva. Mom told us we should not miss the Red Cross Museum. She told me that the Red Cross helps people live healthy and good lives and also helps in emergencies. I remembered seeing the American Red Cross asking for donations for earthquakes in other countries., and I learned that the center for all Red Cross organizations is based in Geneva, Switzerland.

It was up on the little hill, and as we entered the building, I saw a big board that had letters sent to different places by different soldiers during the war. Things that were used by the Red Cross were also displayed. It was really an interesting place. I saw videos and pictures of broken legs injured by bombs. And I thought about wars and how people suffer from them. I wished to volunteer to help the poor and suffering people some day.

I want to volunteer...

Transportation Museum, Luzern—*J.J*

The transportation Museum in Luzern was awesome! There were trains, planes, hang gliders, cars, and everything. The best thing was riding on an old plane. I crashed though. But everything in there was cool. Next time, I want to go there again and spend a whole day there. I even rode a scooter through the exhibitions. It was so special.

So special!

Transportation Museum, Luzern—*R.J*

After eating Raclette and Fondue for the last time in Switzerland, we went on a train to Luzern where we took the bus to the Transportation Museum. There, we got to see old trains, try things out, and tour places with scooters. It was fun to try the different things. Before we left, we put our ticket (sticker) on the beetle in front of the museum. The Volkswagen beetle was already all covered with other people's stickers, but I tried to place mine as noticeably as possible.

Tickets on the beetle!

Lion Statue, Luzern—*J.J*

The dying lion in Luzern has the saddest face on earth. Mom told me about the 360 Swiss guards who died for Louis XVI during the French revolution, and the lion statue is to honor them. I couldn't believe my ears. It was a sad story. The dying lion had a broken arrow through the back. I tried to look at the lion in detail by squinting my eyes, until my mom called me to go. I wanted to be a brave person just like the Swiss guards.

Lion Statue, Luzern—*R.J*

With the beautiful Chapel Bridge behind us, we went to see the Lion Statue. We didn't know exactly where it was, so we just followed a group of tourists. Following the crowd got us to the correct place. When I saw the lion, it reminded me of the Bloody wars the Swiss guards had fought. It had the saddest face I've ever seen. The sculptor made it to memorialize the Swiss guards during the French Revolution.

It shows how brave and sad the 360 Swiss guards were when they protected Louis XVI. Unfortunately, they all died. I thought it was the best monument I've ever seen of. It was on a flat rock surface, which is very unusual and special.

I wondered how the sculptor made it work on the rock cliff. Since our time was up for visiting Luzern, we rode a train back to Zurich to catch the flight to Dubai.

United Arab Emirates

Dubai

Desert Safari Tour

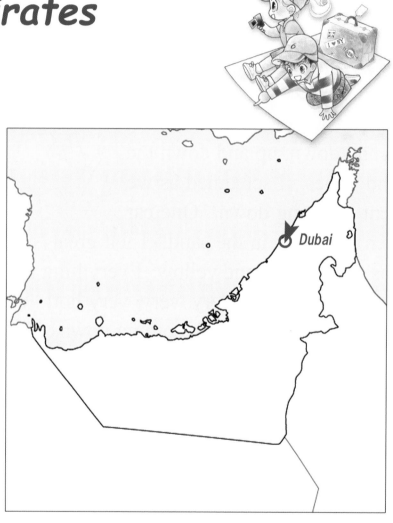

Desert safari tour—*J.J*

Horse riding is so much better...

Scorpion

I was all ready to go to the crazy and wild desert safari tour in Dubai. We zoomed around like we were in a race car. We went up and down, up and down the sand dunes. I screamed as we went zooming down. One car even got stuck in the sand! I felt great 'cause we didn't get stuck. The color of the sand was orange, red, and yellow. Everything was covered in mounds and mounds of sand. The sand was burning, very, very, very hot! We saw the sunset too. The sunset in the desert looked like an egg yolk coming down. The sunset was beauty itself! Then we went to a camp filled with many visitors, especially from America! I tried camel riding and many other things. The camel riding was scary when the camel stood and also when it knelt down. Camels move their butts up high when they stand; you feel like you're falling down. I liked the camel ride second best. Horse riding is the best.

I got a henna tattoo, too. A scary looking women drew a scorpion on my arm! It did not hurt at all. The woman said it would last for ten days. My dad didn't like us trying it. He worried that it would last forever. It was fun, though. I tried to scare my sister with my scorpion. I liked it.

Desert safari tour—*R.J*

We saw Bruj Khalifa on our way to the desert. Our guide began to tell us about this and other famous buildings in town. It was interesting that nobody knew how many stories Bruj Khalifa will be until it is finished. But it will be the tallest building in the world. The buildings in Dubai all looked vacant. When we entered the desert area, we had to wait until everyone in the tour got together. As I stepped out of the car, warm air surrounded me. The dunes were beautiful and soft looking. And the golden sun was about to set behind me. Next we followed the leader to the dunes to ride over them to the place where we would have our snack. The dunes were a natural roller coaster. I screamed with glee while riding up and down them. It was a lot of fun.

After drinking some soft drinks, we went on our way to the camel farm where we saw an Arabian falcon and Arabian goats, as well as camels. Everything was great, but I was disappointed that I couldn't

Golden Sun!

So chubby!

touch the camels. I was told to keep a distance from the camel 'cause they can bite or kick people. Finally, we went to the camp. There were lots of things to do. We got to ride the camels, and I got a henna tattoo, saw a belly dancer, and drank some Arabian coffee.

The henna tattoo was like a pen squirting out mud. My brother got a scorpion, my mom got a flower, and I got a butterfly on my arm. It was so pretty. Tasting different foods and coffees was a lot of fun, too. The Arabian coffee tasted exactly like tea. It felt smooth in my mouth. I liked the belly dancer, but she was chubby and not so pretty. She was very talented at shaking her body. Overall, it was a really nice experience for me.

 # China

HongKong

- Hong Kong
- Sampan Ride
- Dimsum Restaurant

Macau

- Macau

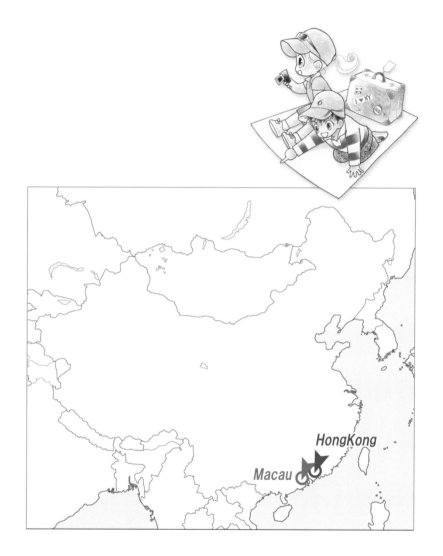

Hong Kong—*J.J*

The marvelous city of Hong Kong! Hong Kong was so convenient. It belongs to China but not like Shanghai. I liked everything except the underground tunnel, which smelled different because of the humidity. Shopping was great in Hong Kong. People speak English. I bought two pairs of Ferrari shoes and Dad bought me my first trumpet. I was so happy I trembled with joy! The sound of the trumpet was low! I liked it a lot. I thanked my dad a million times in my heart.

My First Trumpet!

Hong Kong—*R.J*

As I stepped into the hotel room, I saw a beautiful view of Hong Kong on the other side of the harbor. It was breathtaking. Fresh fruit was on the table, and there was a telescope, too! The room was so nice, we didn't want to leave it. But we decided to explore a bit. We went down to the shops and found a jade shop with a sign hanging on the door that said, "Closed." We were about to turn away when the shop owner came rushing in and opened the door for us. I asked him if he had any loose stones. He brought out a big one and said it was $50. I bought it immediately. When he knew I was buying it out of my own pocket, he gave me a hand made jade bracelet and my brother a jade necklace as well. It was very nice of him.

After that, we walked along the Tsim Sha Tsui area, a famous shopping district. We saw a piano shop and asked if they had any trumpets. Someone told us to go to Tom Lee and marked it on the map. After a short walk, we found the largest music shop I have ever been to. We got a mini trumpet for my brother. He was overjoyed. Hong Kong is a great place for shopping.

Beautiful harbour view!

Sampan Ride—*J.J*

A chubby Chinese lady was driving a boat called a Sampan. She took us to where the boat people live in Everdeen Harbor. Their boats were houses for them. I was surprised to see that they had pets. I saw dogs and cats on the boat. They also had TV and everything they needed, I think. They wove nets to catch fish but the water was so dirty. I thought I was going to puke when I saw a fish. But I liked the decoration of the Sampan boat.

Sampan Ride—*R.J*

I was excited that we were going to Everdeen to ride the traditional Chinese fishing boat called SamPan. I was surprised to see that the boats were run by motors. Mom told me that the boats had not been run by motors in older days. We got to see the famous Chinese floating restaurant called Jumbo.

We also saw the Boat People. They are called Boat People because they live on boats. There were many different kind of boats. Some were very old and dirty, but we saw many clean ones too. The fun part was to see the boat driver's house. The people who had the old boats had two or three of them. The driver had two. My questions were, "How do they take showers? and "How do they pee?" I do not think I can ever live on a boat.

Dim Sum Restaurant—*J.J*

There were millions of people in the Dim Sum restaurant. The servers were busy as bees, but at least the food was delicious. They passed by with a cart full of dim sum baskets, and we pointed out the basket we wanted. Then they passed us the one we picked. My favorites were Sharongpo and Hagau.

Dim Sum Restaurant—*R.J*

We decided to eat lunch at a famous dim sum restaurant called Maxim near city hall. The dim sum was wonderful. It was the best I had ever tasted. I ate a lot. I kept emptying the basket. I thought I would never be able to eat that kind of delicious dim sum again, so I ate as much as I could. For the finale, I had Mango Pudding. It was out of this world. I ate it as slowly as I could, but I did not want to stop eating.

Can't stop eating

Macau—*J.J*

We took a one hour boat ride to a Portuguese Island, Macau, that is now part of China. It was like a mini Las Vegas. I especially liked the golden tree leaves in the Wynn Casino. There was an area near the tree where people could throw coins and pray for a blessing. I found people in China pray first and then throw the coins, but Koreans do the opposite. They throw the coins and then pray. I wonder how Americans would do it. I felt rich just by looking at the tree made with 100% gold.

Macau—R.J

We went on a ferry to Macau. I was excited when I got out after a one hour ride. It was a totally different city than Hong Kong. From the ferry terminal, I could already see a tall tower, casinos, and shimmering buildings. We changed some money into Macau dollars and went into the city with our guide.

First, we saw a kids' playground. We saw the Casino owner's house, the mayor's house, the Portuguese government building, a chapel, and the Wynn Casino, or should I say, mall. I found out that the color pink was the national color of Macau. I saw a lot of pink houses.

The chapel was once a wooden chapel, but a typhoon came while the candles were burning, and it caught fire and collapsed. The only thing that still exists is the wall made of stone. It became the symbol of Macau.

In that village, we tried the Portuguese dessert. The egg tart was so good that I ate two. In Wynn, I saw the gold tree. It was all gold. I couldn't believe it. I learned that the show itself cost about 10 million dollars. It was very pretty. When we returned to Hong Kong, it was past our bedtime. But I really had a fun last day in Hong Kong visiting Macau.

 # Korea

Seoul

Gayaguem Factory

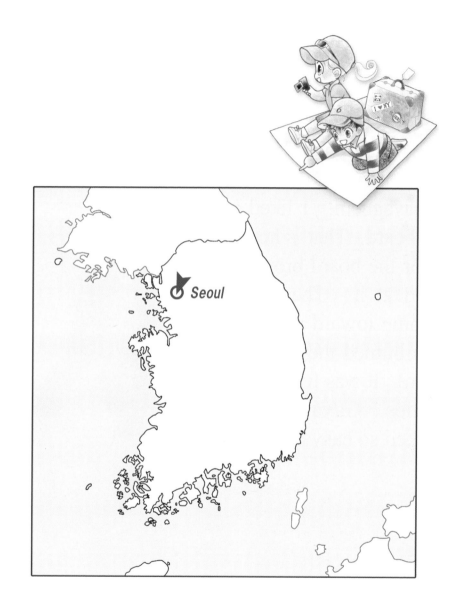

Seoul

Gayaguem Factory, Korea—*J.J*

Mom took us to a Gayaguem factory in Korea. We went there because of my sister. I wanted to stay in Seoul playing golf and swimming. But when I got there, I wanted to stay for the whole day. There were a lot of things to play, such as archery, Korean seesaws, javelins, and a huge drum. I even learned how to make a Gayaguem! I liked ironing the board. That is how people color the board brown. I was good at it. The smoke was coming toward my feet as the iron burned the surface of the board. It was fun to watch the flames. Gayaguem making looked so easy and great fun.

What fun!

Gayaguem Factory, Korea—*R.J*

We decided to go and experience Gayaguem making. It took two hours by train from Seoul to get there. I was excited to see the factory. When we got off, we got into a taxi and headed to the Gayaguem making place. In front of my eyes was the biggest Korean

I love Gayaguem!

fiddle I've ever seen. It was all made of bamboo. For outside activities, they had a big drum we could try out, as well as small drums, mini archery, and a Korean seesaw.

Looking at all the activities made my brother very anxious to try them. But first, we were introduced to some people working there. After meeting them, we were shown the wood carving section. We even tried to carve a wooden piece. They have to keep that piece for five years to dry. Next we were brought to a long narrow room where they did the spinning (braiding) of the silk and nylon thread which is used as string. They did a demonstration for us and we tried it. It was so cool. We held a wooden thing straight and then we pulled while walking with it. After joining a class that taught us about Gayaguem, we tried an iron stick that gives Gayaguem its brown color. It was hard trying to do it correctly, but we enjoyed it a lot. Last, we bought a Gayaguem, and I couldn't wait to learn how to do it.

United States of America

Los Angeles

Los Angeles

Los Angeles

Los Angeles—*J.J*

Yeah!

I am finally back in the States. LA is famous for Hollywood and movies. Every movie nowadays is shown first in Hollywood. The stars on the street were interesting.

They have famous people's names on them. I thought I wanted to be famous someday and see my name on the street, too.

I want to be famous someday!

JIMIN JUNG

Los Angeles—R.J

We arrived at Los Angeles at about 12pm. After we dropped our luggage off at the hotel, we took a town car to tour Beverly Hills, Rodeo Drive, and Hollywood. Beverly Hills was a very pretty place. Movie and rock stars live there. The premium area is called Bel Air. It is hard to see the houses because the trees block them from the street. A famous street with all the famous shops is called Rodeo Drive. We enjoyed shopping, and we also ate there. It was really nice walking down Rodeo Drive.

Next, we arrived in Hollywood where we saw stars on the concrete pavement. Our driver explained that the stars were matched with the names of successful celebrities. Before leaving Hollywood, we went to the observatory to get a view of the entire city. It seemed pretty small from there, but luckily we found a good place where we could take a picture with a panoramic view. I got a souvenir. It was a star keychain that said #1 daughter. I wished I could be #1 daughter to my parents.

Although the tour was only a few hours, I felt like I had toured the whole city when I returned to the hotel.